UNIVERSAL BASIC INCOME IN THE UNITED STATES

Is UBI a Good Idea?

ANDREW SMITH

Table of Contents

INTRODUCTION

Learning About Universal Basic Income

A universal basic income or UBI refers to a guarantee from the government that each of the citizens will receive a minimum income. It's also known as a basic income, citizen's income, or guaranteed minimum income. The intention of this payment is to give the citizens a sufficient amount of money for the basic cost of living as well as to provide them with financial security.

When it comes to UBI, the plans on who will receive the income vary. Some plans would pay each individual citizen no matter what their income is. Other plans only provide payments to the citizens below the line of poverty, whether they are employed or not. Then there are those plans which would only pay the citizens who are unemployed because of robotics or technological advancements. This particular plan is the most popular among Americans as around 48% support it.

The government would send the UBI check, but the source of the income would vary as well. Some of the plans would require a tax increase on the wealthier citizens, while other plans would take their funding from corporations. In this book, you will learn all about the universal basic income. Before you can decide whether or not you support the adoption of a UBI, you need all the basic information first. Read on to learn more about UBI, how it differs from welfare, some studies that have been conducted on it, and the key arguments for and against UBI.

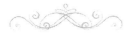

CHAPTER 1

What is Universal Basic Income?

Universal basic income (UBI) is a type of plan or model wherein all citizens of a certain geographic country or area are provided with a specific amount of money regardless of their employment status, income, or resources. The main purpose of this is to reduce or prevent poverty while increasing equality among the country's citizens.

According to BIEN or the advocacy group known as Basic Income Earth Network, the basic principle behind the UBI is that all citizens deserve to receive a livable income regardless of either the circumstances they were born into or their contribution, or lack thereof, to production and society as a whole. UBI comes with a number of defining characteristics which are:

- **Periodic:** This means that the payments are given at regular intervals.

- **Cash payments:** This means that the payments are given to the citizens in the form of funds instead of vouchers for products or services.

- **Individual:** This means that each of the adult citizens will receive the payment, not one payment for each household.

- **Universal:** This means that all of the citizens are entitled to receive the payments.

- **Unconditional:** This means that the recipients don't have to demonstrate a willingness or a need to work in order to be entitled to the payments.

Most of the UBI implementation plans involve identical and periodic payments which are given to all of the citizens of the country. The tax system would ensure that the funds go back to the system through payments made by the citizens who earn higher incomes. Typically, the amount would be determined for subsistence. This means that the amount should cover the basic needs only.

The universal basic income is an example of a model of guaranteed income. The primary alternative model to UBI is known as the guaranteed minimum income or GMI system, which is also known as the basic income guarantee or BIG. This model involves different supplements which are based on needs. The design of this model ensures that all of the citizens possess enough money for them to live on.

The idea of guaranteed income was introduced by Thomas More in his book titled *Utopia*, published in 1516. At the time, the Renaissance was ushering in the idea that caring for the poor was the job of more than just the church and individuals inclined to be charitable. Since then, proponents of UBI have included a number of famous people such as Abraham Lincoln, Thomas Jefferson, Martin Luther King Jr., Chris Hughes, Mark Zuckerberg, Franklin Roosevelt, and Margaret Mead. With all these big names behind the concept of guaranteed income, it's no wonder people are still pushing for UBI hundreds of years after the idea was first proposed.

Today, UBI is being considered as a way to support the workforce that will be displaced because of automation and the advancement of technology. Zuckerberg, Elon Musk (co-founder of Tesla), and others have expressed the belief that software enhanced by artificial intelligence and robots may quickly replace most of the human labor workforce in the near future. They refer to this future scenario as the "robot economy." The displaced workforce is likely to increase poverty rates, which may likewise increase demand for a UBI.

However, the critics of UBI and other guaranteed income models argue that the implementation of the model would be too costly. They also argue that providing people with a UBI that has no strings attached will cause those individuals to lose their motivation to work.

On the other hand, the proponents of these models believe that, in the long-run, UBI is actually cheaper, especially when the impact of poverty is being considered. The argument can also be made that a UBI can potentially promote entrepreneurship and creativity among the citizens who are liberated from their constant struggle to survive.

How Much Would Universal Basic Income Cost?

For many people when they first learn about UBI, it seems like an excellent idea, especially to those who are progressive. After all, providing a livable income to all people would increase the quality of life and decrease poverty levels. However, this model does have two main flaws:

- There are very high odds that the effort to secure UBI would be impractical.

- There is a high certainty that the possibility of being able to overcome the obstacles of UBI would need a left-right coalition with conservative support which, in turn, might actually increase poverty instead of reducing it.

Yes, UBI seems extremely appealing, but how much would it really cost?

Right now, there are more than 300 million American citizens. Suppose the universal basic income would provide all of these citizens with around $10,000 each year. Multiply this with the number of citizens, and UBI would cost over $3 trillion every year. Over ten years, the total amount would range from between $30 trillion to $40 trillion!

The one-year figure would already be equal to over three-fourths of the total annual federal budget, and it would be twice as large as the whole budget with the exception of spending on defense, Medicare, interest, and Social

Security payments. The amount is also almost equal to the entire tax revenue amount collected by the federal government.

So, what if we lower the amount? Let's say that UBI would provide each citizen with $5,000 each year. This will provide income to the citizens equal to around two-fifths of the poverty line for each individual or less than the poverty line for each family with four members. However, the cost would still be the same as the whole federal budget outside defense, interest, Medicare, and Social Security payments.

Some proponents of UBI respond to these facts by saying that the policymakers should make the payments of UBI taxable. Despite this, the savings to be made would be fairly modest since most of the citizens in America are either in the 10% to 15% tax bracket or they don't owe any federal income tax.

Let's say, for instance, that all of the 328 million American citizens receive a UBI of $10,000. The total cost would amount to $3.28 trillion each year before taxes. If they make these payments taxable, this would only reduce the total cost by between $2.5 trillion to $2.75 trillion.

Now that we've come up with an estimation of the cost, where would this huge expense come from? Of course, it's not possible to take the whole amount or even a majority of that amount from taxes. As it is, we still need new substantial revenues for the next few decades in order to maintain the solvency of Medicare and Social Security so as to avoid cutting large benefits from them. In order to take UBI from taxes, the government would have to increase taxes further, which, in turn, impedes the country's economic growth.

Also, in order to reduce racial barriers, create more opportunities, and lower inequities, there will be a need to put up new revenues for the purpose of investing more in other areas such as child care, preschool education, college affordability, and so on. A UBI which primarily comes from taxes would mean that Americans would have to deal with a taxation level that significantly exceeds anything which has been done in the history of the country.

Who Pays for Universal Basic Income?

Recently, there has been a renewal of interest in UBI where cash payments would be given to all citizens regardless of need, race, or gender. Some of the most famous people in history were proponents of this idea, and even now, it's quite popular among such people as well, including Mark Zuckerberg, Peter Barnes, Carole Pateman, George P. Schultz, and more. Today, the interest has surfaced once again because of the income stagnation that the working poor and the middle-class citizens of America have experienced along with the persistently slow growth of the economy.

Nowadays, the wealth gap in the US is widely increasing. Because of this, there are several arguments saying that now is the perfect time to distribute the country' wealth in order to maintain social peace. The idea of UBI is supported across the ideological spectrum of America in this era when not many ideas get bipartisan support. Some liberals see this as a way of preserving the middle class since they don't receive enough compensation from their jobs now. Some conservatives like the idea because they see it as one way to reduce our dependence on the Byzantine welfare maze.

The wide appeal of UBI comes from the fact that each and every citizen in a particular country, state or locale will be able to receive the same amount just enough to cover basic living costs. Although universal income is a promising concept, there's still the matter of who would be paying for it. The good news is that we can also use our universal assets (such as land, digital assets, creative output, and so on) or commonwealth to pay for this universal income.

The wealth inherited and created by Americans amounts to trillions, but presently, we are able to derive almost nothing from it. This joint inheritance consists of fresh water, minerals, our atmosphere, and other priceless gifts of nature along with assets which have been socially-created like our financial and legal infrastructure. For the proponents of UBI, they believe that this is where the funds may come from. But when it comes to who will be paying for UBI, we don't just have to consider a single source. This is the beauty of a universal income. It can actually be derived from four different sources, namely:

- **Current spending**

Currently, the country is spending between $500 billion to $600 billion each year on food stamps, disability, welfare programs, and more. All of these reduce the cost of UBI since people are already being provided with benefits, and if these continue, such people might not be eligible to get the whole amount in addition to their current benefits.

Furthermore, the country is already spending more than $1 trillion on homelessness services, incarceration, health care, and more. As a country, we may be able to save up to $200 billion if people take better care of themselves so as to avoid going to jail, the emergency room or ending up on the streets. This, in turn, would make people more functional, too. UBI would be able to pay for itself as it helps people avoid institutions since this is where the costs are really high.

- **A VAT**

Right now, the American economy is huge, being worth $19 trillion as it went up to $4 trillion in just the last 10 years. A value-added tax (VAT) would be able to generate up to $800 billion for new revenue. This becomes more significant with the improvement of technology because it's not possible to collect income tax from software or robots.

- **New revenue**

Giving the money back to American consumers helps the economy grow. One study conducted at the Roosevelt Institute projected the growth of the economy at around $2.5 trillion while creating up to 4.6 million new job opportunities.[1]This, in turn, would generate around $800 to $900 billion in new revenue thanks to economic activity and growth.

- **Taxes on pollution and top earners**

When the Social Security cap is removed, a financial transactions tax is implemented, and the favorable tax treatment for carried interest or capital gains is ended, we may be able to reduce financial speculation while funding Freedom Dividend. Add to this a carbon fee wherein part of it goes into the Freedom Dividend and we will be able to cover the remaining balance needed to cover the UBI's costs.

For instance, consider our atmosphere's limited capacity to absorb all of the pollutants causing climate change. If we charge anyone who pollutes the atmosphere, we will be able to protect it while generating dividends for the citizens too. Then there could be similar prices for those who pollute the planet in other ways. When extractors and polluters are tasked to pay, there would be market-based incentives for everyone to start respecting nature.

---

[1] More information on http://rooseveltinstitute.org/wp-content/uploads/2017/08/Modeling-the-Macroeconomic-Effects-of-a-Universal-Basic-Income.pdf

Can We Afford Universal Basic Income?

Proponents of UBI claim that it can help eliminate poverty, reduce inequality, and allow for more financial stability in a nation of precarious work. Simply giving enough money to everyone so they can sustain themselves each day helps make the country a better place. In fact, the same study at the Roosevelt Institute we mentioned in the previous section showed that providing a UBI amounting to $1,000 each month in America has the potential to increase the gross domestic product (GDP) by up to 12%. This is because it allows poor people to spend their own money, which, in turn, increases the overall demand.

As simple as this concept may be, it does have a major issue. A lot of supporters and even some critics don't really understand the cost which means that they don't really know if we can afford a UBI. In order to understand UBI's actual cost, we need to understand the difference between net or "real" cost and gross or "upfront" cost. Let's look at an example to illustrate this:

For instance, there is a group of 15 people who would like to create a UBI of $2 for each person. The gross cost for this policy would amount to $30. Ten of the richest members of the group would be required to provide $3 each toward the UBI fund. After contributing this amount, they are able to raise the required $30. Because of this, each person in the group receives their $2 UBI. However, since ten of the richest members of the group had given $3 each and they got $2 back, their net contribution amounts to $1 each. Therefore, UBI's real cost in this example is $10.

This is how you can come up with the real cost. So the question remains, can we afford it?

People should understand who will actually gain money through the UBI and who will contribute to it. The net contributors would also get a UBI, but before this, they would be contributing the UBI amount which they will receive plus a specific amount on top of that. Basically, this means that the people who will be taxed to pay for UBI will also get some of that payment back in the form of their own UBI.

The same thing goes if UBI is taken from other sources, not just from wealth or income taxes. If data assets or corporate taxes are used or if carbon or natural resource taxes are implemented to finance the UBI, the money would still be redistributed. This means that the money won't just go to a smaller group of people. Rather, more people would benefit from it. As confusing as this may be for some, the bottom line is this: As long as those in charge of planning, sourcing, and distributing UBI use careful consideration and planning, America can actually afford it. But the question is, who can be in charge of it to ensure its success?

Would People Still Do Hard, Boring, or Unfulfilling Labor?

At the surface, UBI seems like a very tantalizing idea. However, there's more to a UBI than simply receiving the payments regularly. Those who don't agree with the implementation of UBI believe that because people will be receiving regular cash payments, they won't strive for more as they settle into a life of having enough. But this argument has been debunked in a huge way by a recent study which examines the impact of universal basic income in Alaska's population. [2]

For the past 25 years, the Alaska Permanent Fund Dividend has been in existence. The funds come from royalties earned by the state from oil reserves. Each resident of Alaska receives yearly unconditional cash payments. The results of the study showed that any potential reductions in terms of employment are offset by

---

[2] More on https://home.uchicago.edu/~j1s/Jones_Alaska.pdf

the increase in spending which, in turn, increases employment opportunities. Basically, the researchers discovered that these payments didn't have any real negative or positive impact on the levels of full-time employment of the residents. However, they did discover a 17% increase in part-time work.

Although this is just one study, the results are significant. The increase in part-time work may be an indication that some people had, in fact, left their boring, unfulfilling, and difficult jobs in lieu of easier, more interesting ones where they didn't have to spend the whole day at work. However, since the levels of full-time employment didn't change, this may mean that as these people left, they were also replaced by others who want to move forward in their career.

Last year, the banks of Wall Street provided their employees with over $26 billion in bonuses. This amount alone would be sufficient to provide payments for all American citizens working full-time at the current minimum wage. Employees of Wall Street enjoy these bonuses, but according to the Standard Economic Multiplier Model, if the minimum wage were to be increased, this would give the country's economy a significant boost. In order for minimum-wage earners to meet their basic needs, they need to spend all the money they earn while the wealthy can afford more while still being able to save a portion of their earnings.

All of the dollars spent by minimum-wage earners create a ripple effect on the economy. With a wage increase, each extra dollar that goes into the pockets of these low-wage employees would add approximately $1.21 to the national economy. By contrast, each dollar that goes into the pockets of high-income citizens only adds around 39 cents to the national economy. In this situation, if the bonuses of Wall Street employees would go to the minimum-wage workers instead or if the money would be used for a UBI, it would be more beneficial to the economy.

Proponents of the UBI also claim that eliminating welfare would save a lot of money. When these benefits are removed, the government agencies in charge of providing them would cease to exist as well. Of course, since we are already so used to the concept of welfare and since so many people rely on it, removing this might leave people worse off than they were before.

Think about it: If you were to receive basic cash payments each month, does this mean that you would leave your daytime job? Maybe you would have the courage to change careers or move from one job to another because you would have a safety net. Or you might feel more confident in terms of negotiating for a higher pay or better working conditions. But in the end, most people would still choose to keep working in order to sustain their lifestyles or to add to their income so they can move forward in life.

CHAPTER 2

Universal Basic Income Versus Welfare

The main difference between a universal basic income and welfare is that the former isn't meant to control the decisions of people below the poverty line. UBI isn't conditional, which means that it won't stop coming if a person won't get a job, doesn't have a disability, moves from a full-time to a part-time job, or basically makes any significant changes in his life. UBI is a specific amount of cash which allows poor people to spend it however they wish instead of forcing these people to purchase specific items such as food or rundown apartments.

It isn't surprising that the concept of UBI is very popular among left-wing liberals and libertarians. The latter doesn't want governments to be in control of the populations' behavior while the former doesn't perceive poverty as the main issue of why poor people behave the way they do.

However, one possible disadvantage of UBI as compared to welfare is that poor people might not know how to spend the money they receive wisely. A lot of them drink more frequently, have children out of wedlock, don't actively search for employment, are high school dropouts, purchase lotto tickets in hopes of getting a break, and perform a lot of imprudent behaviors. Therefore, in the case of most poor people, their causality works both ways - their poverty pushes them to make bad decisions and their bad decisions cause them to remain poor.

But in the case of welfare programs, the benefits here are only offered to certain types of people. Aside from this, there are certain guidelines which must be followed in order to remain on the welfare program. This means that welfare doesn't really provide equal opportunities to everyone. This is why people believe that it controls the behavior of poor people... because it does!

Welfare Typically Comes with Strings Attached

Right now, the welfare system isn't really able to address the issue of poverty, but it's not because there is a lack or an absence of resources. In 2016, for the first time in over 40 years, there was a national increase in benefits and in 2018, there were benefits allocated which excluded superannuation amounting to more than $13 billion. But still, poverty exists. It's clear that the problem with welfare isn't because there's a lack of spending. So how can we solve this problem?

The main issue with the current welfare system is that it's too extreme. Before people can receive welfare, they must meet the strong requirements with regards to their values and character. This value-loaded approach comes with significant economic and social downsides. For one, this approach has a tendency to restrict labor mobility because those who depend on the community to survive can't just move away in order to pursue employment opportunities.

In order to be eligible for welfare, the recipients should prove that the income they earn is below a specific amount. For 2019, the amount is $25,750 for a family with four members. In the US, there are some main welfare programs, and they come with their own requirements:

- **Temporary Assistance for Needy Families or TANF**

For this program, families must prove that they are below the poverty line in order to receive benefits each month. The amount given depends on the state and the number of family members. However, despite the monetary assistance they get, these families still live in poverty.

Additionally, in order for a family to be part of this welfare program, they have to find employment within 2 years. In cases where there is an addition to the family, such as the birth of another child, they may receive more money. They have to own assets worth $2,000 and below. Finally, in some states, families can only receive TANF for a maximum of five years.

- **Medicaid**

This pays for the healthcare of low-income adults and children from low-income families. It pays for about 40% of all births in the US, health expenses for disabled and blind people, and for low-income seniors.

- **Child's Health Insurance Program or CHIP**

Apart from Medicaid, children are eligible to receive benefits from this program. It provides children with preventive care as well as medical tests, medical supplies, and hospital care.

- **Supplemental Nutrition Assistance Program or SNAP**

This is more commonly known as food stamps. On average, a person receives food stamps valued at around $126 each month. For people without children who receive this benefit, they have to find employment after three months. However, this requirement is waived for people who live in areas which have a high rate of unemployment.

The Special Supplemental Food Program for Women, Infants, and Children, which provides benefits to young children, pregnant mothers, and nursing mothers, falls under SNAP. There is also the Child Nutrition Program which provides reduced-cost or free lunches to children.

- **Supplemental Security Program**

This welfare program is for individuals with vision impairments and other disabilities, as well as the elderly. They are provided with a certain amount of money each month for their clothing, shelter, and food.

- **Earned Income Tax Credit**

Families who have at least one child are eligible for this program. The EITC refers to a refundable credit for those who earn moderate to low incomes. Anyone who is eligible for the EITC can either increase their tax refund or reduce their taxes. This means that individuals and families are able to keep more of their money. There is also a specific income amount (that changes each year) which they must fall under in order to qualify.

- **Housing Assistance**

Here, units of public housing are made available to specific individuals. Qualified individuals are provided with rent certificates. In some cases, families can also use the voucher to buy a small home.

As you can see, people must meet specific requirements in order to be eligible for certain welfare programs. If you don't fall under these but you also happen to be poor, what then? How can the country eliminate the issue of poverty if the programs come with strings attached?

Why Welfare Isn't Ideal

Apart from not providing equal opportunities to everyone, welfare actually has the tendency to encourage laziness, thus trapping people in their own poverty. In the US, the government offers welfare programs in order to ensure a standard of living for each person. Usually, these programs are focused on children to ensure that they will have enough clothes and food to survive. Although welfare programs are meant to do good, this isn't always the case. Here are some reasons why welfare isn't an ideal option:

- **There is a possibility of fraud**

There are some cases where such programs are exploited. To prevent this, the government may need a special group or body to take charge of investigating each case of welfare. This should help reduce the risk of giving help to those who just want to cheat the system.

- **It tends to make people dependent on hand-outs**

Since people will be able to receive money even without working, and this may encourage dependence. The whole system tends to create workers who are less motivated because they have gotten used to the feeling of receiving money without earning it. Such people would then prolong their unemployment for as long as they possibly can. During this time, their skills and knowledge would start deteriorating which, in turn, makes them less qualified to work.

- **It might discourage people from getting married**

Finally, people who receive welfare might not want to get married because then, their incomes would be added together. If their combined income goes beyond the target amount for eligibility, this means that they won't be able to receive benefits any longer. Therefore, such people would choose to remain single so the money would keep coming.

Although welfare can be highly beneficial to some people, it doesn't seem to be a long-term solution. People who receive these benefits still live their lives in poverty. They have gotten so used to these benefits that they don't feel motivated to find jobs to take themselves out of the welfare system.

UBI Can Never Be Cut

One good thing about the UBI is that it can never be cut. You would receive payments regularly no matter what you do and no matter what situation you're in. Unlike welfare where you would need to fulfill certain requirements, the UBI would be given to everyone. For some people, this would be their main source of income. But for others, they would use this amount as a supplement to the income they are earning from their jobs.

However, despite all the worries of those who are against the UBI, several studies have already proven that UBI won't really have a significant impact on workforce participation. The reason for this is that, to most people, their work isn't just about the money they earn. People choose to work as it supports their sense of human dignity and identity. Although they would be receiving a steady paycheck through UBI, this won't be enough to push the majority of the population to simply give up the careers they worked hard to build.

Although some people may resign from their jobs, this won't be because they would feel satisfied with the money they receive. In most cases, these people would find part-time work in order to supplement the UBI. For other people, they would choose to stop working in order to contribute to society in different but equally meaningful ways. For instance, mothers who need to care for their children or those who need to care for the elderly members of the family would have the freedom to do so if they were to receive a UBI. Although they aren't earning an income from that type of work, they are still doing something important with their lives.

Probably one of the biggest benefits people look forward to is the fact that they will be given a choice. They don't *have* to work because they will be receiving a set amount to cover their living expenses. But for those who want more, they can *choose* to work in order to sustain their current lifestyles.

Of course, all of these arguments are only arguments because, in the US, a UBI is still a long way off. However, it's always a good idea to learn more about concepts such as this so that if ever they become a reality, you will know what to expect and how such a huge change would impact your life. The question is this: If the US government would choose to implement the UBI, would you choose to stop working or would you stick to your career?

CHAPTER 3

Will Universal Basic Income Cause Inflation?

When it comes to UBI, this is one of the most common concerns. A lot of people worry that if a UBI is given to everyone, this might cause the prices of basic commodities (and other items) to inevitably increase. Although the idea of giving a universal basic income to all citizens is a noble one, if it leads to inflation, then it would be quite pointless. Poor people still won't be able to afford anything even though they would receive regular payments. However, would a UBI really cause inflation?

In order to come up with the money for a UBI, the government won't have to print new notes. The money would come from what already exists in the current economic system. This means that it won't be new money; it would simply shift from one place to another. Therefore, this also means that the value of dollars won't go down either. The money would only change hands.

Aside from this, it's also important to note that although the money supply would be vastly expanded because of a UBI, the impact on prices doesn't have to be extreme. In fact, the effect might even be the exact opposite, meaning, we might even experience deflation. It would be much easier to see and understand the impact of UBI on inflation by using some examples:

• UBI in Alaska and Kuwait

Back in the year 1982, residents of Alaska had started receiving a partial UBI each year. At the time, the state had a higher inflation rate compared to the rest of the US. Because of the introduction of the first dividend, Alaska experienced a lower inflation rate compared to the rest of the US.

The residents of Kuwait also received a partial UBI amounting to $4,000 back in the year 2011. There was a fear of inflation because of this, especially since the country already had a high inflation rate. However, this move actually improved their rate of inflation because it decreased the rate from more than 9% to below 4%.

- **Variables of supply and demand**

Another way to understand this better is to learn about the variables of supply and demand in terms of goods and services. When demand exists and supply has already been paid for, it's unlikely for demand to change since UBI would simply be a replacement method of payment. For instance, providing a UBI instead of giving food stamps won't push people to purchase more food. Instead, they would probably purchase the same amount, only this time, they would be using cash. In such a case, it's unlikely that inflation would occur.

- **The issue of rent**

In addition to the threat of a price hike on basic commodities, a rise in rent is also something people worry about. But when it comes to rent and housing, you must remember these two things:

- ○ Right now, there are five times more vacant homes than homeless people in the US. This means that there is a huge housing supply that remains unused because people can't really afford to rent or purchase homes. But if all people are given a UBI, more people would be able to afford accommodations.

o If everyone receives regular payments each month, they will be able to afford rent. However, since they should budget this amount for other things as well, these people would look for cheap places. Because of this, renters would have to lower their prices in order to stay competitive. And in such a situation, those who offer the lowest prices would be victorious.

These are just a few examples of the unlikelihood of inflation if a UBI exists. The fact is, inflation is a complex equation which involves several variables. Just because all of the citizens in a certain country or area will be given a basic income, this doesn't necessarily mean that inflation would occur soon after. In fact, when you look at the evidence, it shows that there's not much to fear when it comes to this particular issue.

Won't Prices Go Up?

There is no definite answer to this question as it all depends on how the UBI will be implemented. Typically, prices would go up when demand would exceed the supply levels.

Labor is a necessary and valuable resource. Therefore, an incentive for labor should exist. In America, when you take into account all of the labor hours then divide this number evenly between all of the able-bodied adults between the ages of 20 and 65, you will get a value of approximately 30 hours of labor for each person per week. However, if people stop working because they receive a UBI, this would be an issue because it would cause a reduction in the supply of this resource (labor).

In order to fix this issue, there should be an increase in the incentives for labor. Either that or there may be a need to tax a specific amount of money from the system, however, this would mean a reduction in the net income of some workers. Although this wouldn't have much of an impact on the upper-class, it would have a significant effect on the middle and lower-class citizens.

Probably a better solution to this issue which would ensure or at least lower the risk of a price hike would be to increase demand in such a way that supply also increases. For instance, the government may provide a UBI to everyone while also offering a program which guarantees employment. In such a situation, people would receive guaranteed money while also increasing demand. There would be an increase in supply as well coming from the increase in the labor force (from the guaranteed jobs). Since the increase in demand is offset by an increase in supply, prices would not change.

Although this is just an example, it does show how the implementation of a UBI can affect inflation or the increase in prices. This is why the concept requires a lot of planning and careful consideration. The pros and cons of a UBI must be taken into account in order for the implementation of it to go smoothly and to be beneficial for the majority.

CHAPTER 4

Empirical Case Studies of Universal Basic Income

Across all of the emerging and developing economies, leaders are always searching for ways to reduce poverty and income equality. The good news is that in the past century, both poverty and extreme poverty have significantly declined all over the world. Recent studies have shown that since the year 1900, poverty around the world has decreased from approximately 85% to around 50% in the year 1990. Now, this number has dropped to less than 10%. In the case of extreme poverty worldwide, 2019 started with less than 8%, which is the lowest prevalence ever recorded in the world's history. A lot of people credit this decline to the worldwide increase in capitalism and free markets.

One possible solution to reduce or eliminate poverty in this century is to provide a universal basic income or UBI. This concept is similar to some of the social security systems which already exist in different countries including the US. The main purpose of a UBI is to provide a minimum income for all of the residents regardless of willingness or performance at work. This concept has already been suggested in several contexts as a "market socialism" model and as a model of free market capitalism. But how effective is a UBI? Let's take a look at some empirical case studies conducted about UBI from places where it has already been implemented.

Case Study 1: India

Our first case study comes from India, a country which has an abundance of villages and communities, most of which qualify as extremely poor based on global economic standards. Various regions in India have already proposed the UBI system several times, and some of them have already implemented their own UBI systems. In the year 2011, a project was launched in Madhya Pradesh known as the "Madhya Pradesh Unconditional Cash

Transfers Project" in cooperation with UNICEF. The goal of this project was to reduce poverty and economic disparities.

Over a period of 18 months, 6,000 residents in this rural region received a UBI. Each of the adults received an amount of 300 rupees each month while each child received an amount of 150 rupees (approximately $2.16). Several studies were conducted over the course of this time period to compare how the villages that received a UBI fared compared to those that didn't receive any kind of financial aid.

One of the major findings from this project was the increase in the number of children enrolled in schools in different villages. Thanks to the UBI, there was a higher level of enrollment of both male and female children in the villages that received UBI compared to those that didn't receive anything.

For instance, children between the ages of 14-18 had a school enrollment level of 76% in the villages that received a UBI while the school enrollment level was only 51.3% in the villages that didn't receive a UBI. The UBI villages also experienced an increase in their income-earning by 21% while the increase was a mere 9% for the non-UBI villages. These were some of the most significant improvements seen by the researchers in a study conducted back in 2012.[3]

Case Study 2: Alaska

In the year 1976, Alaska's State Constitution created the "Alaska Permanent Fund" or APF. This amendment came after a rush on oil where drilling leases generated around $900 million in revenue. Clearly, this commodity wouldn't be an infinite source of money for Alaska's residents, so the state decided to create the APF to set aside revenues.

In the year 2014, the state provided each of their "year-round citizens" with a UBI amounting to $1,884 annually, which was their share from the $6.8 billion net income of the APF. To qualify for this amount, a resident must physically reside in Alaska. Aside from this, the person should have taken a step to establish residency in the country before January 1 of the qualifying year. This person should also be able to provide evidence of their intent to reside in the state indefinitely. This dividend

---

[3] More information on
https://basicincome.org/news/2013/08/india-basic-income-pilot-project-releases-an-impressive-list-of-findings/

came from the net income and was given to 640,000 of Alaska's citizens. Since then, the amount of the UBI given to the residents of Alaska has fluctuated mainly depending on the current oil prices. In the year 2015, oil prices were high so the residents received a UBI of $2,072 each. But in the year 2017 when oil prices were low, the amount of their UBI went down to $1,100 per person.

Despite the amount of the UBI received by the residents, one of the most notable effects (or lack thereof) of this system is that it didn't result in fewer working residents. A comprehensive study conducted in 2018 showed that despite receiving cash payments regularly, the employment rate in Alaska didn't change significantly.[4] However, they did notice an increase in the levels of part-time work after the implementation of the UBI. Still, it seems like, at least in Alaska, basic income didn't push them to choose unemployment just because they were already earning money from the government.

Of course, it's important to note that the UBI scheme in Alaska is quite unique since they do have their own fund which is financed by the revenue earned through oil. Unfortunately, not all states or countries have such a fund,

---

[4] More information on
https://home.uchicago.edu/~j1s/Jones_Alaska.pdf

so they would have to come up with their own income sources.

Case Study 3: Canada

In the year 1974, the government of a province in Canada, Manitoba, started one of the biggest and most significant social experiments in the history of the country. This social experiment was called The Manitoba Annual Income Experiment or "The Mincome Experiment" for short. This was one of the very first implementations of the UBI system that was applied to the whole population.[5] Therefore, it serves as a very rare example of how a UBI impacts both individual and community incomes. This experiment was triggered by a growing concern and institutional awareness over the proliferation of poverty in Canada. To solve this issue, the provincial government of Manitoba started the Mincome Experiment as a new way of facilitating welfare.

The main objectives of this experiment were to evaluate the country's economic situation, identify challenges in logistics, and to understand the ramifications of a UBI. As

---

[5] More information on http://www.lse.ac.uk/LSEE-Research-on-South-Eastern-Europe/Assets/Documents/Events/Conferences-Symposia-Programmes-and-Agendas/2018/FORGET-MINCOME-and-Ontario-short.pdf

they investigated new mechanisms for the facilitation of welfare, the government of Canada wanted to assess the social and economic consequences of an alternative system (UBI) based on the idea of a negative income tax. Specifically, they focused on what this entails for the outcomes of labor supply.

Many of the studies focused on how the UBI affected Dauphin because this was considered a "low-income" town; therefore, the residents here would be the ones who would feel the most prominent effects of receiving a UBI. Within this town, all of the 586 families were provided with a total of 3,800 Canadian dollars each year (approximately $2,880). These families received the UBI for about three years. After this time, the funding was canceled after the researchers completed their collection of data. Several factors contributed to this abrupt cancellation of the program, one of which was the high inflation rate which occurred throughout the 1970s.

The results of this study showed a small effect on the labor markets as working hours dropped to 3% for married women, 5% for unmarried women, and 1% for men. However, for this particular implementation of a UBI in the town of Dauphin, social researchers and economists didn't see the experience of the residents as useful in their analysis. Still, this was one of the most significant experiments conducted which focused on a UBI even though the system doesn't exist in the country anymore.

Case Study 4: Finland

The government of Finland has been providing a guaranteed UBI to 2,000 unemployed residents each month with no strings attached. This is another robust experiment focused on the UBI, and some of the early results seem to be in favor of this controversial concept. UBI can be implemented in different ways, but the basic idea behind this is to provide everyone with a consistent and guaranteed income enough to cover all of their basic needs; the amount of this UBI must be the same for everyone.

This experiment started in December of 2016, and it was conducted by Kela, Finland's Social Insurance Institution.[6] They selected 2,000 people at random between the ages of 25 and 58 from all around the country who were receiving unemployment benefits. The researchers replaced the benefits received by these people with a guaranteed UBI

---

[6] More information on https://www.kela.fi/web/en/basic-income-experiment

amounting to 560 euros each month (approximately $637). Whether these people choose to find a job or not, they still received the monthly payments. This experiment ended on December 31, 2018, and Kela had already released the preliminary results. They compared the employment status, general wellbeing, and income of the people who received the UBI with another group of 5,000 people who continued to receive unemployment benefits.

Preliminary results showed no significant difference between the number of employment days in the year 2017 of both groups as they shared the same average of 49 days. Those who received the UBI earned 21 euros less (approximately $24) compared to the other group in the year 2017. In terms of stress and health levels, those who received a UBI perceived an improvement in these levels. Although these are just the preliminary findings, this experiment serves as a significant stepping stone toward being able to understand UBI and its effects better in real-life applications.

Case Study 5: Namibia

In January of 2008, the first official UBI system was launched in one of the villages in Namibia called Otjivero and it was called the Basic Income Guarantee or BIG.[7] This pilot project was launched with the purpose of convincing the federal government of Namibia about the benefits of a UBI to social policy. The funding of this particular project came from both international and national sponsors who are presumably connected with the BIG Coalition of the country. It's important to note that the federal government didn't have any contribution to the funding of this project as it has consistently dismissed the potential and the results of such a concept.

Empirical studies about this project are limited to assessment reports which have been published by researchers of the Namibian BIG Coalition in the years 2008 and 2009. In January of 2008, each of the 1,200 residents living in Otjivero was provided with a UBI for a period of two years after which, the amount of the payments was significantly reduced. Only those who were over 60 years of age didn't receive this UBI because they were already receiving state pensions. The residents received 100 Namibian dollars (approximately $7) a month. After two years, the UBI was reduced to 80 Namibian dollars (approximately $5), but in the year

---

[7] More information on http://www.bignam.org/BIG_pilot.html

2016, it was halted because Namibia's federal government officially rejected the idea.

After the conclusion of the experiment, there were some significant findings which came out. For one, the BIG project encouraged community empowerment and mobilization. Since this project was only introduced in a single location, the researchers noticed a significant migration to this location as they were attracted by the prospect of receiving a guaranteed UBI. Also, there was a significant drop in household poverty after the BIG project was introduced. This was one of the more notable results as it showed that such a project may have a significant impact on the country's poverty levels.

Another change they saw was an increase in the area's economic activity. The project enabled the people who received the UBI to increase their productivity at work for profit, family gain or pay as well as for self-employment. The UBI also enabled the people to increase the productive income they have earned, specifically by starting their own businesses. It also made a contribution to creating a local market as it increased the buying power of households. These results show how such a program won't necessarily lead to dependency and laziness.

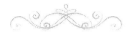

CHAPTER 5

Key Arguments Against Universal Basic Income

In order for anyone to make a sound decision about anything, it's important to look at both sides of the story, and the UBI is no exception. Simply learning what a UBI is won't really help you determine whether you agree with its implementation or not. We've already gone through the fundamentals of UBI along with a few of the most significant studies on it. Now let's look at the key arguments for and against the universal basic income. Knowing about these arguments will give you a better understanding of the UBI and why some people are strongly for it and why others are strongly against it.

First, let's go through the arguments against a UBI. Since this concept seems extremely promising, especially to the middle and lower-class citizens, you may wonder why countries all over the world haven't started implementing it yet. For one, if all of the welfare programs were to be replaced by a single payment system, the government would have a lot of leverage and power. Also, individual welfare programs would be easier to cut or attack as compared to a single UBI. Here are other arguments against UBI:

It's Costly

The supporters of UBI claim that this is a very efficient replacement for the already bloated welfare system. They believe that providing a UBI would actually lower the overall costs. However, if the UBI comes from the state, this means that it would still be a welfare state, just with a different name. Therefore, the UBI would just be another costly replacement for one costly system. Unlike the current system of welfare in the US, which comes with its own standards for the determination of who would qualify for the benefits, a UBI would be provided to *all citizens*. Therefore, this dramatically increases the number of people receiving the benefits which, in turn, inflicts huge expenses overall.

This disadvantage remains a reality if the entire source of funding for the UBI were to come from the state or from the government. However, the situation may change if the funds were to come from a number of different sources. In such a case, having a UBI system in place may be a more realistic possibility. Then again, since everyone would receive the UBI, the country would definitely require a constant source of income to keep the program going. But if the country were to struggle or plunge into debt because of it, having a UBI isn't really a viable option.

It's Financially Irresponsible

The next key argument from those who are against a UBI is that it may lead to financial irresponsibility. But what exactly does this mean? Think about it—the term "universal" means that everyone would get it. Therefore, even in societies that are rich, if they set a UBI at a level which provides everyone with a decent yet modest standard of living, this won't be affordable. It may also result in ballooning deficits. In order to prevent the UBI budget from becoming a financial "black hole," the government must increase the taxes. Either that or there should be a reallocation of resources from education, health, and other areas.

Then there's the possibility of a UBI resulting in higher poverty and inequality. Typically, the aim of this concept is to replace other kinds of benefits with a simpler universal payment. But when welfare payments are relocated from their targeted transfers—such as housing, unemployment, or disability benefits—to a universal transfer which everyone receives, the amount received by those who really need it becomes lower while those who are already rich also receive the same amount thus making them a bit richer. This is why a UBI isn't considered a financially responsible system.

Incentives Are More Effective Than Handouts

For a lot of people, the main downside of the UBI is that it's a handout just like welfare benefits. When people receive handouts, they might lose their interest in finding work, especially for those who are satisfied with just having enough to get by. Conversely, giving incentives would be more beneficial. There is no greater incentive than having a job that provides financial security. Earning money through hard work is a lot more motivating than receiving something like a UBI which, sadly, a lot of people would take for granted.

Although a UBI would benefit a lot of people, especially those below the poverty line, some people might lose their financial incentive to find work. Those opposed to a UBI see this as a way of the government inadvertently encouraging idleness which, of course, is never a good thing. In America, the entrepreneurial spirit is deeply woven throughout our people's history. But the introduction of a UBI might weaken this spirit, especially if it's not implemented in the right way. At the end of the day, it's always better to have an incentive to keep working to keep us highly motivated to look for a job and work hard to keep it.

It Reduces the Social Aspect

Another downside of implementing a UBI is that it may weaken social cohesion. When people work, they earn money as well as status, networks, skills, friendships, and meaning through their work. They build a professional life which becomes an important aspect of who they are. But when you break the link between work and income by paying people even if they don't work, this may lead to social decay. More and more people might choose to resign from their jobs, especially if they're not happy with what they are doing. When this happens, the likely outcomes could be a rise in crime, broken families, drugs, and other things that are socially destructive.

In addition to losing the incentive to work, a UBI might also weaken a person's incentive to participate. It's important to have strong safety nets, and no respectable society should accept starvation or dire poverty. However, for able-bodied adults, any help they receive should encourage them to participate in their society. When the UBI would serve as their safety net, some people might not want to find meaningful work nor would they choose to be an active member of society. Instead, they would simply rely on the payments they receive, which, over time, causes them to live a life of dependence.

The Welfare State Won't Be Going Anywhere

Finally, those who are against a UBI also claim that having this might reform, decrease, or even abolish the entire welfare system. However, nobody seems to know how this would actually happen. The reason for this is that there is no existing transitory plan for such a system. If such a plan were to come to fruition, this may lead to the political suicide of whoever proposes it because there's always the risk of angering the wrong group of people. For those politicians who depend on the approval and support of their own constituents, such an idea is sure to be met with unwanted criticism.

Anyone who has experience creating policies knows that even suggesting the elimination of Social Security and welfare benefits is a surefire way to alienate people, especially the older generation. As a matter of fact, if you just mention that there's a chance that these benefits would decrease, you would most likely get an uproar. Even if you propose a different plan—such as a UBI—this won't be enough to calm the apprehensions and fears of these people. This is especially true when they think about having to go through the period of transition from one system to another. Because of this, most people believe that a UBI won't really work, because the welfare state really won't be going anywhere.

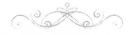

CHAPTER 6

Key Arguments For
Universal Basic Income

Although there are a few key arguments against UBI, there are also some key arguments for it. In itself, UBI is a promising concept. Imagine how much of a relief it would be for people to receive regular payments to cover their basic living expenses. This is especially true for those who live below the poverty line and for those who are always struggling to make ends meet. They don't have to worry about where their next meal will be coming from, as long as they budget the amount they get each month so they can buy everything they need for themselves and for their families.

UBI is not a new concept but in recent years, it has caught the attention of people all over the world and for good reason. Some countries and areas have already tried implementing their own version of a UBI system, and most of these have experienced positive results. UBI has a lot of proponents because of its potential and because of the main concept behind it. So let's take a look at some of the key arguments for UBI to give you a clearer understanding of why a lot of people support it and are interested in it.

It Reduces Poverty

Although some people believe that a UBI might even increase poverty, there are several studies which have contradicted this. Back in the year 1981, Alaska's rank on income inequality was #30 out of the 50 states. But by the year 2015, the state ranked second! This huge improvement in terms of income equality has been largely credited to their implementation of a UBI system which began in 1976 (Case Study 2 in Chapter 4).

The UBI system of Namibia called the Basic Income Grant (BIG) also reduced the poverty rates from a whopping 76% down to a mere 37% after just one year (Case Study 5 in Chapter 4). Aside from this, the rates of child malnutrition had also dropped from 42% to 17% in a matter of 6 months.

These are just some examples of how a UBI can actually reduce poverty when implemented well. This is why Scott Santens, a proponent of the UBI and one of the founding members of the Economic Security Project, claims that giving a UBI of $1,000 each month to adults and $300 to children each month can potentially eliminate poverty in the US entirely. Of course, we can only speculate on how this would go. We will only be able to see the real impact of a UBI in America if the government actually chooses to implement a system for it.

Promotes the Efficient Utilization of Natural-Resource Rents

Natural resource rents refer to the money earned by a country from their natural resources such as forest rents, soft and hard coal rents, natural gas rents, mineral rents, and oil rents. Most countries that are rich in oil are located in the sub-Saharan areas of Africa. Unfortunately, these countries, including Equatorial Guinea, Gabon, and others, suffer from poor outcomes in terms of public spending.

For instance, these two countries have per capita incomes of only $10,000 to $20,000. one of the main reasons why they're so poor is that the oil revenues their countries earn go straight to their governments. None of these revenues pass through any of their citizens. Therefore, the citizens don't even know how huge these oil revenues are. Even if they do know about these oil revenues, they either don't think that it's "their money" or they don't feel like there's anything they can do about how their governments spend the money.

But if these oil revenues are given to the citizens of the country, they will know the magnitude of the oil revenues. Giving them a small percentage of the oil revenues can potentially eliminate the issue of poverty in oil-rich countries. Probably the best example of using natural resources efficiently to allow for a UBI is in Alaska with the Alaska Permanent Fund. The government of this state actually set aside the oil revenue in order to provide a UBI to the residents and this move has, indeed, resulted in positive changes.

It Encourages Positive Career Growth

The guaranteed income from a UBI actually keeps people protected from low wages, sluggish growth in wages, and the constant problem of unsure job security. Even if a person would be stuck in a low-paying job, he would still be receiving the UBI which adds to his monthly income. A lot of times, people don't feel motivated enough to do their work well because they feel that they are being underpaid. But if they receive such an incentive from the government, they won't have to feel like they're struggling financially. Because of this, they can focus more on their work and on becoming a more productive employee in the workplace.

One of the key arguments against UBI is that it might cause people to lose interest in working or in finding work. However, this doesn't always have to be the case. If people don't have to worry about not having enough money to sustain their lifestyle, they may have a more positive outlook on their work. They would feel more motivated to push themselves harder in order to move forward in their careers. Money won't have to be an issue anymore, therefore, they can focus on how fulfilling their jobs are, what they can do to climb the corporate ladder, and even find the joy in the job which they previously saw as nothing but a burden.

Allows for Adjustments to Labor-Saving Technologies

This benefit of a UBI is geared toward the future. Advancements in robotics, AI, and other kinds of labor-saving technologies have started to call into question the future of manual labor. The problem is that when these technologies start replacing humans in the workplace, people will inevitably lose their jobs. How will they earn money to support themselves and their families?

The management of this particular transition is a huge challenge from a moral, economic, and political viewpoint. One program that might relieve some tension is a program or system where a part of the productivity increase gets taxed and that tax money is then given to all of the citizens as cash payments whether they are employed or not. The tax is called a productivity tax, and an example of that type of tax is when technological devices or equipment increase productivity in a company, therefore bringing in more income, so the company has to pay a higher tax because of their increase in productivity. Such programs and systems are already being proposed and piloted in a few countries such as New Zealand, Switzerland, and Finland. Although we have yet to discover the outcomes of these programs, these countries are challenging the fundamental idea that you can only earn money through work.

Although the concept of a UBI has been in existence for some time, this is the perfect time to revisit the concept of UBI in light of all the changes and advancements in technology. In a society where productivity is at its peak and each citizen receives a UBI, people won't have to worry about losing their jobs or finding work that they love or that they are really good at.

It Guarantees Income, Especially for Women

The final argument (although there may still be others) is that a UBI would guarantee income, especially for women. Since this income would be given to everyone regardless of their gender, age, status, or more, it means that nobody is exempt. This is important, especially in countries where women aren't given the same opportunities as men in terms of employment.

Apart from this, the UBI is especially significant for women because of how most of them live their lives. When a woman gets married and gives birth to children, the issue of raising those children becomes a reality. Nowadays, both parents are forced to work in order to support their children. And the more children a couple has, the more income they must generate. But with a UBI, women won't have to work in order to support their children. When they get pregnant, they don't have to worry about not being able to get back to work after giving birth. This means that they can focus on raising their children while still being able to add what they receive to their family's budget.

And if the UBI program also includes giving cash payments to children, parents can set this money aside for their future education. When you look at the UBI this way, you can see why it's an excellent concept and why it does have a lot of people supporting it.

CONCLUSION

Making a Wise Choice

There you have it, all you need to know about the universal basic income or UBI. This is a simple concept that has been around for years but that has never been implemented by any country as a permanent system. Just like any other financial concept, UBI comes with its own advantages and disadvantages. The more people learn about the UBI, how it can potentially affect a population, and how it has affected those which have already tried implementing it, the more they can determine whether it would be suitable for their own country or not.

Before any government can make a decision to implement some kind of UBI system in their country, state, or area, they must consider several factors. Having a UBI will surely be beneficial for everyone but only if it is implemented in the right way. Making a wise choice involves planning, careful thought, and looking at all the possible outcomes of this decision.

Now that you know all about the UBI, you can start thinking about how you would feel if your government started to consider implementing UBI. Although this might not be part of America's near future, having knowledge about the UBI arms you and prepares you for any kind of situation which may arise.

REFERENCES

Amadeo, K. (2019). 6 Major Welfare Programs Myths Versus Facts. Retrieved from https://www.thebalance.com/welfare-programs-definition-and-list-3305759

Amadeo, K. (2019). Should Everyone Get a Guaranteed Income? Retrieved from https://www.thebalance.com/universal-basic-income-4160668

Anderson, S. (2014). Wall Street Bonuses and the Minimum Wage. Retrieved from https://ips-dc.org/wall_street_bonuses_and_the_minimum_wage/

Basic Income Grant Coalition - Namibia. (2019).
Retrieved from
http://www.bignam.org/BIG_pilot.html

Boyce, J., & Barnes, P. (2016). How to Pay for Universal
Basic Income - Economics. Retrieved from
http://evonomics.com/how-to-pay-for-universal-
basic-income/

Brown, C. (2019). With Strings Attached—The case for
welfare with expectations. Retrieved from
https://medium.com/@camryn.brown/with-strings-
attached-the-case-for-welfare-with-expectations-
2fac3a046fd5

Copeland, J. (2018). Universal Basic Income: More
Empirical Studies. Retrieved from
https://sevenpillarsinstitute.org/universal-basic-
income-more-empirical-studies/

Devarajan, S. (2017). Three reasons for universal basic
income. Retrieved from
https://www.brookings.edu/blog/future-
development/2017/02/15/three-reasons-for-
universal-basic-income/

Dodge, J. (2016). Universal basic income wouldn't make people lazy–it would change the nature of work. Retrieved from https://qz.com/765902/ubi-wouldnt-mean-everyone-quits-working/

Establishing Residency. (2019). Retrieved from https://pfd.alaska.gov/Eligibility/Establishing-Residency

Experimental study on a universal basic income. (2019). Retrieved from https://www.kela.fi/web/en/basic-income-experiment

Forget, E. (2019). The MINCOME Project and Ontario's BIG Experiment. Retrieved from http://www.lse.ac.uk/LSEE-Research-on-South-Eastern-Europe/Assets/Documents/Events/Conferences-Symposia-Programmes-and-Agendas/2018/FORGET-MINCOME-and-Ontario-short.pdf

Fouksman, E. (2018). Universal basic income costs far less than you think. Retrieved from https://qz.com/1355729/universal-basic-income-ubi-costs-far-less-than-you-think/

Gaskell, A. (2019). Does A Universal Basic Income
Discourage Work? Retrieved from
https://www.forbes.com/sites/adigaskell/2018/03/05
/does-a-universal-basic-income-discourage-
work/#757d1d08541b

Global poverty: Facts, FAQs, and how to help | World
Vision. (2019). Retrieved from
https://www.worldvision.org/sponsorship-news-
stories/global-poverty-facts

Goldin, I. (2019). Five reasons why universal basic
income is a bad idea | Financial Times. Retrieved
from https://www.ft.com/content/100137b4-0cdf-
11e8-bacb-2958fde95e5e

Greenstein, R. (2019). Commentary: Universal Basic
Income May Sound Attractive But, If It Occurred,
Would Likelier Increase Poverty Than Reduce It.
Retrieved from https://www.cbpp.org/poverty-and-
opportunity/commentary-universal-basic-income-
may-sound-attractive-but-if-it-occurred

How would we pay for Universal Basic Income? (2017).
Retrieved from
https://www.yang2020.com/blog/ubi_faqs/pay-
universal-basic-income/

Howgego, J. (2019). Universal income study finds money for nothing won't make us work less. Retrieved from https://www.newscientist.com/article/2193136-universal-income-study-finds-money-for-nothing-wont-make-us-work-less/

Hugill, J., & Franklin, M. (2017). The Wisdom of a Universal Basic Income. Retrieved from https://behavioralscientist.org/wisdom-universal-basic-income/

Hunter, B. (2017). The Top Three Arguments against a Universal Basic Income. Retrieved from https://fee.org/articles/the-top-three-arguments-against-a-universal-basic-income/

Jones, D., & Marinescu, I. (2018). The Labor Market Impacts of Universal and Permanent Cash Transfers: Evidence from the Alaska Permanent Fund. Retrieved from https://home.uchicago.edu/~j1s/Jones_Alaska.pdf

Kharas, H., Hamel, K., & Hofer, M. (2018). Rethinking global poverty reduction in 2019. Retrieved from https://www.brookings.edu/blog/future-development/2018/12/13/ rethinking-global-poverty-reduction-in-2019/

Kuwait: Keeping on. (2011). Retrieved from
https://oxfordbusinessgroup.com/news/kuwait-keeping

Lombardo, C. (2019). 6 Advantages and Disadvantages of
Welfare. Retrieved from
https://futureofworking.com/6-advantages-and-disadvantages-of-welfare/

MADHYA PRADESH UNCONDITIONAL CASH
TRANSFER PROJECT. (2019). Retrieved from
http://unicef.in/uploads/
publications/resources/pub_doc83.pdf

Matthews, D. (2018). The amazing true socialist miracle
of the Alaska Permanent Fund. Retrieved from
https://www.vox.com/policy-and-politics/2018/2/13/16997188/alaska-basic-income-permanent-fund-oil-revenue-study

Nikiforos, M., Steinbaum, M., & Zezza, G. (2017).
Modeling the Macroeconomic Effects of a Universal
Basic Income. Retrieved from
http://rooseveltinstitute.org/wp-content/uploads/2017/08 /Modeling-the-Macroeconomic-Effects-of-a-Universal-Basic-Income.pdf

Oswald, J. (2016). Basic Income vs. Welfare. Retrieved from https://azmytheconomics.wordpress.com/2016/07/14/thoughts-on-basic-income/

Roy, A. (2016). Universal Basic Income: Empirical Studies. Retrieved from https://sevenpillarsinstitute.org/universal-basic-income-empirical-studies/

Santens, S. (2014). Wouldn't Unconditional Basic Income Just Cause Massive Inflation? Retrieved from https://medium.com/basic-income/wouldnt-unconditional-basic-income-just-cause-massive-inflation-fe71d69f15e7

The Earned Income Tax Credit. Qualifications for EITC. (2019). Retrieved from https://www.efile.com/tax-credit/earned-income-credit/

Total natural resources rents (% of GDP) - SCO. (2014). Retrieved from https://competitivite.ferdi.fr/en/indicators/total-natural-resources-rents-of-gdp

Universal Basic Income - Top 3 Pros and Cons. (2017).
Retrieved from
https://www.procon.org/headline.php?headlineID=0
05363

Witcher, S. (2019). Won't a universal basic income raise
inflation? Retrieved from
https://www.quora.com/Wont-a-universal-basic-
income-raise-inflation

Made in the USA
Middletown, DE
27 September 2019